FLIRT

by the same author

SIMPLE MEN
TRUST
AMATEUR

FLIRT

Hal Hartley

faber and faber

LONDON · BOSTON

First published in 1996
by Faber and Faber Limited
3 Queen Square London WC1N 3AU

Photoset by Parker Typesetting Service, Leicester
Printed in England by Clays Ltd, St Ives plc

A CIP record for this book
is available from the British Library
ISBN 0-571-17954-1

2 4 6 8 10 9 7 5 3 1

CONTENTS

Preface by Tom Gunning, vii
Introduction by Hal Hartley, xi
FLIRT, I
Credits, 89

THRICE UPON A TIME:
FLIRTING WITH A FILM BY HAL HARTLEY

> But you know, everyone really only makes one film in
> his life, and then he breaks it up into fragments and
> makes it again with just a few little variations each time.
>
> Jean Renoir

Is it ever possible to repeat oneself perfectly, to re-enact a gesture, a statement, a scene – even a memory – as an exact duplication? The flow of time never cycles back perfectly. The same statement takes on different meanings, an act reverses its effect, and even when history does repeat itself, it changes from tragedy to farce in the rerun.

But what about cinema? Wasn't this technology invented so that time could be embalmed, captured once and for all in an endless loop of repetitions and continuous showings? *Flirt* dissects the paradoxes of repetition and transformation, creating a film that is at once an experiment (hence a discovery), a demonstration (hence a proof) and a game (hence an entertainment). Rarely has a film-maker let us into the processes of inspiration provided by formal choices so candidly. Before our very eyes Hartley shows the way an image and a sound, a character and an environment, a story and a situation, all transform each other through rearrangement and juxtaposition. But *Flirt* is no classroom lecture, no laboratory distillation. Like all of Hartley's films, *Flirt* is filled with passion, humor, regret, mystery and, ultimately, miracle. In *Flirt* we see how the encounter between a contingent reality and a situation that demands a definite decision gives birth to a film – to three films, in fact, and to one total film, which is these three films interacting and playing together. And the passion and miracle comes from the fact that for Hartley it is not only films that are born from sudden encounters between random acts and final commitments, but love and life itself.

A flirt, Hartley shows us, is a creature who dwells in ambiguity, who skates along the edges of a definition and breathes in the gap

vii

between the question and the answer. Hartley's films are always made up of shots (exquisitely realized by cinematographer Michael Spiller) with well-defined borders, composed within the rather narrow focal plane of a 50mm lens. His dialogue consists of hard-edged witticisms and ironies that circulate from character to character and situation to situation. He is a director of control and precision, a film-maker who believes (as did Hitchcock, Bresson and Lubitsch) that there is truly only *one* proper place in which to put the camera, one viewpoint which reveals the drama. And yet, at the same time, he is also a director who shows how the drama changes, goes out of focus, realigns and redefines itself, when another perfectly precise angle of view is chosen. Hartley defines the borders of his shots in order to let chaos move about freely at the edges. Again and again in a Hartley film violence breaks in from the edge – a sudden punch, a lunging body, a slap – sometimes a kiss. Within the carefully arranged world of witticisms, precise gestures and choreographed movements, surprise is generated as a repeated line finds a new inflection in an altered context, or the soft focus background action suddenly invades the sharp and clear foreground. Hartley's order exists in order for the chaos to become incisive and more pointed, as lives are disrupted, families break up and . . . lovers find each other. Because it is also just beyond the very precisely defined edges of his shots that miracles occur.

All of Hartley's characters play games, and he, as director, plays along with them. But at turning points the characters discover their games are larger than they thought they were, and not always as amusing, either. No single person can determine the game. Even the rules can change suddenly. The rules simply allow endless variations of play. In *Flirt* Hartley makes the rules of the game diagrammatically clear for us, the audience, and invites us, as viewers, to play along as we watch. As we note each reoccurrence of dialogue and situation and each rearrangement and new turn in meaning they invoke, we ourselves move through the carefully laid out courses of a Hartley story. From story to story we discover along the way the renewals and transformations that have occurred in the pattern. But, remember, these are more than simple diversions and variations. The game opens itself up again to miracles, as, with each reoccurring disfigurement, the flirt encounters new dimensions of both failure and possibility.

Hartley seems to conjugate all the possibilities of flirt, in gender, race and sexual orientation, and the futures glimpsed by each character (as they confront the explosion that occurs between possibility and decision) varies from story to story. In one story an opening can be created in a moment that in the previous story seemed firmly shut down. A line that reeked of aggression in one story becomes tender in the next. An answer given in one story responds to an entirely different question in the stories to follow. The game is the place in which freedom and restrictions, desires and defeats, cowardice and commitment change place and interpenetrate – eyeing each other, flirting with disaster and with the possibility of true love.

Watching the first two stories, 'New York' and 'Berlin', we catch on to the carefully structured contrasts. The New York flirt flaunts his sensitivity, yet tries to seduce every girl he meets. The Berlin flirt displays his insouciance, flipping through magazines as people pour out their hearts to him, but also repulses each new come-on as if he were already on the road to commitment. The stakes in the game are raised when the struggle over the handgun switches from a bar-room sparring between two males to a domestic loft space under the uncomprehending eyes of a small child. The final decisions in each story are unspoken, expressed by frantic action in New York and a strangely calm resignation in Berlin. Yet the final resolution in both stories remains suspended; we must imagine the outcome of each flirt's next action.

By the time we get to Tokyo, the rules have changed. The game is still going on, many of the pieces seems familiar, but new configurations take place. What is seen and what is spoken get rearranged, as the invisible becomes tangible, the word takes on flesh. Hartley lets us in on this by staging a prologue of sorts, in which we see not only gestures but the director's hand as well; the process of rehearsal and preparation within the world of professional performers. The players are introduced from the start as part of a grand design as we see them positioned and instructed. The incidents in Tokyo become more public, glimpsed by panicked passersby, even investigated by the police. This is a story with little privacy and with a constant awareness of being witnessed, through a doorway or around a corner. As in a dream (which rearranges the events of a day into unexpected juxtapositions, exposing the tensions hidden beneath the familiarity of everyday life), lines we recognize pop up unexpectedly, scenes are split in two, actions are given to new characters. Behind it all we sense the urgency of the film itself, finding its way, stumbling into detours, opening up new pathways in the labyrinth of Tokyo streets. Like the reel of film which in one scene turns in the editor's hand in the foreground (as we hear lines that were the initiation of the drams in the previous stories, now muffled and nearly invisible in the background) the movie takes on its own momentum. Each cut seems momentarily to lose the thread, then to rediscover it, woven into an even tighter web.

Like all great story tellers, Hartley traces the exchange of objects and affections. In *Flirt* we watch guns and film cans and caresses move from hand to hand. In the Tokyo story the shift of objects, lines of dialogue and emotional alliances seems to expand beyond the story structure into a game of urban hide and seek, a cops and lovers quest, whose energy pulses with a growing confidence as it nears the end. Here the visions of the body's past pleasures (which help the flirt endure the pain of the present as her shattered face is stitched together once again), are shown in images, as if all the words have been exhausted. And this sequence, and the film itself, ends as the flirt nuzzles beside the exhausted film-maker, finding rest and perhaps the trust that makes closeness and wordless gestures possible. The game comes full cycle, from the film's opening image of rising from the bed in New York City to this weary nap snatched in a dreary waiting room in Tokyo. If by the end we haven't truly glimpsed the future, we've nonetheless cycled through its permutations, arriving at lovers who – miraculously – have met again.

Tom Gunning 1996

ACTUALLY RESPONDING

Dissatisfaction has a lot to do with why I work. I want to see something and although I look around for it, I can't see it. So I make the thing I desire to see.

Flirt is an exercise. It's like a school assignment and I hope it's entertaining because of this. Only through exercise can I constantly rediscover what I should do with this medium of film: that is, in general, to make work that provides evidence of a personal manner of feeling and which utilizes the actual capacities of the medium.

Recently, a dance magazine asked me to write something about movement on film. I tried and failed. How could I write about it? It seemed pointless. I wound up writing a poem. A poem's plastic reality is much more like the reality of film, which is editing. So I chose to show movement on film (in the magazine) by using words as surrogate images. I juxtaposed them in the way I would juxtapose shots in a movie. It could have been a better poem, I think, but at least I tried.

One evening I was discussing some work I was doing with my friend Travis Preston when he sort of offhandedly said: 'Yes, your work has never been that concerned with subject matter.' I had never heard that notion expressed before. It excited me. Till then I had just felt a kind of impatience with my work: an impulse to stretch back and snap through some confining wrapper of 'completeness'. From the very start I've always been interested in making films that reveal themselves to be aesthetically and philosophically complete; mechanisms of a kind, composed like a piece of music. I began to think this on-going pursuit could lead nowhere but to a body of work that kept the subject matter appropriately 'back'. But now I felt the completeness could be born of the actuality of making the film. And the wrapper would snap.

Mondrian once said a wonderful thing to a friend: 'I don't want paintings, I just want to find things out.' I've got to keep that in mind. He also said: 'The natural does not require a specific representation.' This from an abstract realist. Is that possible in film, abstract realism?

'The subject matter of a film is only a pretext. Form, much more than content, touches a viewer and elevates him.'

Robert Bresson

NEW YORK CITY

I made a short film in New York City in February of 1993 called *Flirt*. I was already planning to shoot *Amateur* later that year and knew I would be editing it on a computer. So I thought of this short film as an opportunity to learn about what editing a movie on a computer was like.

I wrote the film quickly, pulling its parts together from some older, obsolete screenplays, and in the summer of 1992 I produced a version of what is now the New York bathroom scene as a ten-minute play for the Cucaracha Theater in New York City. In that version two young men consult three mysteriously articulate young women – Elina Lowensohn, Adrienne Shelly and Parker Posey. We shot the film in three days and I edited it over the next few months, coming and going between script revisions of *Amateur*.

As we were shooting, I playfully suggested to Mike Spiller, my cameraman, and Ted Hope, the Producer, that we could make this little story many times and in many ways. There was something so typical, common and general about the piece that I felt sure it could be interpreted again and again, always to new effect. It would be exciting to see what would happen if the 'flirt' was a girl instead of a guy, or a gay man, a lesbian, an older person, a child, etc.

Ted and Mike liked the idea and were excited by the suggested attitude of making the same story more than once. But it was forgotten as we moved ahead and made *Amateur* that summer. After *Amateur*, Ted came up with the idea of travelling around the world to make the different versions. He was, at that time, always cooking up these schemes to raise money and travel. It was a good idea and I said yes.

The cities of Berlin and Tokyo were chosen largely because the money came from those places. Chance had a lot to do with it and I encouraged that kind of thing. I wanted to pit my skills and interest against contingency, the random arrival of circumstance.

The thing to remember about *Flirt* is that the three films were made very much as three films, each one separated from the next by almost a year. Each film was completed before I even moved on to making the next.

THE RULES OF THE GAME

Flirt/NYC was an attempt to make shots that were independent of each other; to break the confines of continuity, and to tell a story in film without the need to match everything in one shot with the shot that intercuts with it. I wanted to avoid 'covering' a scene. I wanted each shot to have an autonomy undiluted by the needs of other shots, whether I intercut them or not.

I maintained a sort of scientific detachment from the film, mostly, I guess, because Steve Hamilton, my Editor, and I were, in fact, doing research: figuring out how to edit with the new computer technology. But I liked this approach. I was detached from the footage and passionate about the editing. *Flirt* isn't necessarily concerned with being dramatic. It says the obvious without too much emotional pitch: people (in this case, men) often want more than they should reasonably want and kick and scream when they're forced to choose between one thing and another.

For me, it was like reciting a particularly apt passage of a traditional text. I remember writing the action and telling myself to 'go through the motions': do a desperately jealous husband the way a guitarist might want to cop the sound of a famous Hendrix solo. Of course, a cover never sounds like the original. And why should it?

It's the storyteller's particular interest in *telling* a particular story that makes it compelling. His or her personal manner of feeling. It might be anything – sentimental, perverse, obscure, mean-spirited or fanatical. But it has the chance to be particular. That's all I really expect from creative work. So there's this paradox: the more particular, the more personal, a piece of work is the more it reminds us of our common humanity. Because we compare. We compare ourselves to this peculiar sensibility.

From the film-maker's point of view, it's not so much about 'expressing one's self' as you would imagine. It's more about conveying one's impressions. For me, I try to look. Look through the abstractions of conventional seeing. What is very often referred to as quirky, offbeat or deadpan, is usually just an unjudged image of life; the mundane, everyday character of the obvious but unseen. And I do this because, ultimately, I want to entertain people.

BERLIN

I was familiar with Tokyo. I had been there a few times and knew that if I were to make a reinterpretation of *Flirt* in Japan, it would be the one in which the flirt was a girl. In terms of the scope of *Flirt*, the position of a woman in that culture interested me more than that of a man.

But I knew nothing about Berlin. I knew I wanted to make one version in a gay milieu. So I discovered two general facts about Berlin: it still has a thriving art scene – particularly painting – and it is (and has been for a long time) a popular place for gay men to live. I started from these two generalizations and applied the existing script to them.

The Berlin 'rewrite' was pretty close to the New York version: literally a reorganization of the dialogue to fit a homosexual situation in Berlin – the original idea. But when I got to the part where Dwight addresses three strangers I hit a wall. I could no longer just transpose. The advice given to Bill in New York, repeated again to Dwight in Berlin, seemed to ignore the subtle differences the earlier dialogue had already acquired by virtue of the transposition. So, although there was a crisis, something *was* working: the dialogue and plot *were* acquiring new meaning as a result of the transposition. This crisis proved it.

So the rules of the game became these: I could move scenes around; I could delete lines of dialogue, but not add new ones; I could assign lines of dialogue to different characters. The three strangers in each city would introduce new commentary. And, just for variation, there would be a new recitation in each city.

This type of crisis focused my attention more firmly on the actual circumstance of making the film; using that circumstance as raw material became my method. The film seemed inescapably to be heading towards the 'actual'. It was being made of the materials I had at hand. It reversed my usual production approach. Instead of imposing a design on the circumstances, I let circumstances dictate the opportunities for my design. My part was to respond.

So the three strangers became philosophers (inspired by the name of the street I was living on, Kantstrasse) and I let them dissect Dwight's situation, more or less detailing my own fears in regard to continuing this film. Their arguments lead to an analysis of what my intentions were and what my chances of making a halfway interesting movie might be. The philosophers became construction workers because I was trying to imagine a likely threesome to come upon in a location like that.

That scene, that crisis, made everything possible again. There is always a way. But I have to find it. As for the results, I think I was more successful at some points than at others. But that's an interesting aspect of this movie too. My failures arc just as interesting as my successes because I don't promise anything other than that I will struggle with the rules of the game to the best of my ability.

TOKYO

I now had two pre-existing scripts and two edited films: New York and Berlin. The way in which I needed to scour them for new applications of dialogue, action and scene structure caused me to emphasize activity and woke in me the desire to make a silent film.

Firstly, I removed any dialogue that I thought related an incident through conversation and chose instead to show the related incident. For example, in New York and Berlin the flirt relates how he kissed the married person. When asked how, Bill (in New York) responds: 'She and Walter had had a fight. She was upset. I got her a drink. She cried on my shoulder. I told her a joke. We kissed.'

In Berlin, I was already moving towards activity as an answer. When asked 'how', Dwight just jumps forward and kisses the curious man. Nevertheless, the incident was still only referred to. In Tokyo, I decided to show the incident. So, now I was required to show the object of the flirt's desire (the married person they kiss).

It was in decisions like this that I found the cracks that provided me with the opportunities to make new films out of the same basic script. I had already shown Dwight's heart-throb, Werner, but in a way I would call objective. Werner's actions can in no way confirm or contradict Dwight's suspicions; there is really no way to tell if Werner is interested in the young American.

In Tokyo, if I were going to show the kiss, I would have to decide how this kiss appears. Does Miho kiss the teacher? Does the teacher kiss Miho? Do they kiss each other? What if in Tokyo the 'flirt' was not even flirtatious?

A safe generalization about Japan is that the way things appear is important. From packages to the way one says hello, presentation is everything. I saw the possibility of a comedy of errors firmly anchored in how things appear. I tried writing a silent script, but I couldn't do it. It necessitated too many infractions to the rules of the game.

Being in the film seemed like an appropriate next step once I made the conversation between the three philosophers/ construction workers in Berlin. They discuss the relative success or failure of my whole project. The film-maker's presence is acknowledged; an actuality of the film. The last step was to make the presence real. I didn't really like being before the camera. And I didn't act. I just did things and recited the dialogue. But it was a good idea. Necessary. But I didn't like it. I can't see anything from there.

The Japanese choreographer Yoshito Ohno worked with me on the opening 'rehearsal' sequence of the Tokyo section. Miho had worked and studied with his father, Kasuo Ohno, for about four years and we visited the family home in Yokohama.

I described the film and its story to Yoshito. I described certain ideas for movement, activity; the notion that Miho would somehow be operated by these 'furies' to comfort Yuki (Chikako Hara). Then I described what I wanted the dance rehearsal sequence to convey.

A week or so later, Yoshito came to the first rehearsal in Tokyo with the six male dancers and showed me three short pieces he had put together. I responded more strongly to some parts of each than to others; meaning, certain movements and attitudes lent themselves to the film's story and mood and others didn't, although they were quite interesting in themselves.

We isolated these movements and began to incorporate the two main actresses (Miho and Hara-san). As Yoshito invented and refined movements, I would watch from various parts of the rehearsal hall and get ideas about how to see them. Also, the vantage point would affect the choice of movements. So it worked from all sides. It was not simply a matter of documenting pre-existing movements. The choreography adjusted itself to the frame as well. The finished film contains two of the three main movements. Part of the third is shown as the teacher is directing his wife; he wants her to stand up and look bravely into the future, but she can't.

THEORY AND PRACTICE
I like the definition of flirting I used in the German section. I got it from Toril Mio's book on Simone de Beauvoir: 'chaste amorous relations generally devoid of deep feelings' – which is to say playfulness. I always feel more playful with the shorter films. It makes me think that one can be serious without being deep. Intelligent without being heavy.

I like to imagine that my audience is willing and able to see me stumble and falter sometimes. To see me screw around, tinker, become frustrated, self-defeating, subversive, panicked, provocative, etc. In a word, that they'd be interested in my personal manner of feeling, and, by extension, thinking, discovering, experimenting, questioning. I think I have a generous definition of entertainment.

What I try to remember now is that notions of 'quality' are all relative. I want to be able to go out and shoot and record without preconceived notions of good, beautiful, professional, dramatic, natural, realistic, etc. I want to respond. And this extends to the cutting, story, everything. I want to attain the confidence just to go out and capture images and sounds with the barest of means, then go back and make something out of all this stuff. Let the film evolve out of the collision of qualities in these perhaps disparate images and sounds. I try to avoid submitting to some abstract notion of what a 'good film' is, while remembering to look without preconception. Because even comprehension can be an abstraction, an impediment to seeing. For instance, I could see more accurately when directing actors whose language I didn't share. I could see more readily when they were confused or distracted because I had no choice but to concentrate on their physicality. And their voices, the sound of their voices, is a part of their physicality too. So I watched and listened and was deprived of everything but the outside of these people. Their movements became just movements, their voices became just music. Although, I couldn't speak the language, I almost always saw when they missed a line or said something wrong. Because suddenly they were moving with less confidence and grace. Forty per cent of their mind was now worrying about having screwed up a line a moment before. It helped me see what I'm responding to in film: moving pictures, choreography, rhythm and the musicality of dialogue.

What I find interesting about speech, about dialogue, talking, is that it can be equally compelling by virtue of its success or its failure at communication. Personally, I'm afraid the more I speak the more stupid I become. The less I say the more I accomplish. To this day, I rely less on my intellect than on my emotions, my intuition, my feeling for things. This probably explains my difficulty with computers; I have to use a part of my brain I misplaced over a decade ago.

And I realize my initial attraction to film-making was tactile. All my life I've been more confident and effective with my hands. I wanted to be a carpenter when I was a kid; I couldn't keep my hands off musical instruments and eventually took up the guitar, I painted, etc. The beauty of film machinery alone I found somehow sexy. I have a beautiful old sixteen-millimeter projector still here in the apartment. Editing, filming, threading up the projector, it was all tactile, hands-on and sensual. Frightening too. I didn't trust machines. But I developed a relationship with them.

Now film-making is becoming more and more of an electronic medium. It's excellent technology, I think. But it doesn't attract me in the same way as when film-making was a mechanical medium. I have yet to find the sensuality of the computer. But if I must, I will.

I would like to move towards making films that are in fact more like music; films that can be appreciated the way we appreciate music. When we hear a tune we appreciate, we hum it to ourselves and cannot wait to hear it again. The same with painting, even with theater. But in movies this is popularly reversed. If you have seen a movie once it is usually thought to be exhausted. If it doesn't reveal itself entirely to you in one viewing it is somehow a failure. I would like to make movies that encourage repeated viewings. I like that phrase, attributed to Greenaway, 'infinitely viewable cinema'.

It's becoming apparent to me that, as a film-maker, I think primarily in terms of movement anyway. Even if that movement is very small. A close-up is, for me, still choreographed. I believe that as a storyteller I even conceive of characters physically. I like to know how a character walks, sits, stands, sleeps, etc. before I can write what they say. At this point I'm certain this is because, despite the fact that I love story, character and dialogue, when I isolate the primary elements of film I find photography, movement and sound recording – in that order. Only then do I consider dramatic action.

Film is essentially graphic for me.

Hal Hartley
1996

INT. EMILY'S APT. EARLY EVENING

Bill and Emily have been making love all afternoon. They discuss their future.

EMILY

I feel disgusting.

BILL

Why?

EMILY

I'm a liar.

BILL

No you're not.

EMILY

He writes to me and says he misses me. He calls me and says he loves me. And I reply, 'I miss you too.'
(*turns to Bill*)
But I don't.

BILL

Maybe you don't know what you feel.

EMILY

But I do know what I feel. I love you. Maybe I love him too. But I definitely love you more.

BILL

And I love you.

She sighs and gets off the bed, wrapping the sheet around her as she looks out of the window.

EMILY
(*finally*)
We're using the same language I use when I lie to him.

I

Bill moves to the fridge and takes a swig of Evian. Then:

BILL

What time's your flight?

EMILY

Seven o'clock.

BILL

He's going to meet you at the airport in Paris?

EMILY

Yes.

BILL

What will you tell him?

EMILY
(watching him, then)
What do you want me to tell him?

BILL

I don't want to tell you what to do.

EMILY

Then tell me what you want.

BILL

That would be the same thing.

EMILY
(smokes, then)
It would help me decide.

He turns and looks in at her. After a thoughtful pause, he sighs and looks at his feet.

BILL

He wants you to stay with him in Paris, huh?

EMILY

Yes.

BILL

He wants to marry you?

EMILY

I guess. Eventually.

Emily sits on the edge of the bed. Bill sits down beside her.

BILL

What do you want me to say?

EMILY

I want you to tell me if there is a future for me and you?

BILL

A future, huh?

EMILY

Yes.

She gets up, throws her suitcase on the bed, and starts tossing clothes into it.

BILL

How can I answer that?

EMILY
(*packing*)

Yes or no.

BILL

I can't see the future.

She pushes him out of the way.

EMILY

You don't need to see it if you know it's there.

He takes a deep breath and stands up. Troubled and preoccupied, he glances at his watch.

BILL

What time's your flight?

EMILY
(*packing*)

Seven.

BILL
(pacing)

Seven, huh. OK. It's four now . . .

She keeps packing while watching him pace. He's thinking. He lights a cigarette and stops.

Look. Let me go get Michael's truck. I'll drive you out to JFK.

EMILY

I can take a taxi.

He comes over and takes her by the arms.

BILL

No, I want to. Can you wait here?

EMILY

How long?

BILL
(considers)

An hour and a half.

EMILY

And then what?

BILL

I'll tell you the future.

EMILY
(looks at her watch)

At five-thirty?

BILL

Without fail.

She looks at him and considers.

He seems earnest.

She smiles.

EMILY

Five-thirty.

They kiss.

Bill comes out on to the street, throwing on his coat, and heads for a telephone booth.

He has to wait for the phone because there is a cute young woman deep in conversation. We can't hear what the person on the other side is saying, but the Girl just answers . . .

> GIRL

No.

No.

No.

No?

> *She and Bill make eye contact. She smiles briefly, then is called back to the receiver.*

> (*urgent*)

My time is up. I'll call you right back.

> *She hangs up and searches for a quarter. She can't find one and looks to Bill.*

Excuse me, have you gotta quarter?

> *Bill comes closer, obliging.*

> BILL

Sure.

> *He gives her a quarter. Their hands touch and linger. She smiles coquettishly as she drifts back to the receiver.*

> *Bill leans on the side of the booth, close.*

> *She dials and flashes an apologetic glance at him.*

> *The phone is answered and she continues her conversations, all the while watching Bill.*

> GIRL

It's me again.

No . . .

8

No?
No.
No.
No.
No.

> Bill furtively looks at his watch. He seems to be growing a little impatient. He gestures good-naturedly to the Girl that he's going to go up the street to another phone booth. But she reaches out and touches his hand, urging him not to.

> He stops in his tracks at her touch. He waits and she brings the conversation to a close.

GIRL

OK.
Bye.

> And she hangs up. She stays in the booth and smiles at Bill.

Sorry.

BILL

Don't worry about it.

GIRL

Thank you.

> Finally, she leaves the booth and starts away. Bill steps into the booth, watching her go.

BILL

See you around.

> She glances back at him, flirting.

GIRL

Maybe.

> Bill grins and dials. He waits. Then:

BILL

Margaret?
It's me, Bill.
It's important.

I need to ask you one question.
I want you to tell me if there's a future for me and you?
Yes or no.
You don't need to see it if you know it's there.
Meet me at the bar in ten minutes.

INT. PUFFY'S TAVERN. TEN MINUTES LATER

Bill strides into the bar and approaches the bartender, Mac.

MAC

You owe me money.

BILL

Margaret been in?

MAC

No.

BILL

Let me get a beer, will ya?

MAC

You do owe me money.

BILL

I owe lots of people money.

Mac gets him a beer and slides it towards him. Bill gives him two bucks.

Towards the back of the bar, Bill find his friend Michael, reading aloud from a book.

MICHAEL

'But such hours of worldly delight were followed by others of deepest despondency in which he considered himself eternally damned.'

BILL

Let me borrow your truck. I gotta drive Emily to the airport.

MICHAEL

She's finally leaving you, huh?

BILL
(*irritated*)

Look, she's just going away to France because she's got a job there
for three months. OK?

MICHAEL

You hear the news?

BILL

What news?

MICHAEL

Margaret left her husband.

Bill comes closer, intense.

BILL

You know that for a fact?

MICHAEL

Well, I guess so. I got it from Trish.

Bill pauses and thinks.

BILL

Michael, something happened between me and Margaret.

MICHAEL

Yeah? Like what?

BILL

We got romantic.

MICHAEL

Excuse me?

BILL

Romantic.

MICHAEL
(*considers*)

Romantic.

BILL

We kissed. Once.

MICHAEL
(*realizes*)

Ah, romantic.

BILL

Yeah.

MICHAEL

When?

BILL

A few weeks ago.

MICHAEL

How?

Bill drinks his beer, then sets it down on the bar. He paces back and forth, thinking.

BILL

We are at a party.
She and Walter had a fight.
She was upset.
I got her a drink.
She cried on my shoulder.
I told her a joke.
We kissed.

He stops and looks at Michael.

Michael considers it all, then scratches his head.

MICHAEL

Well, what about Emily?

Bill nods, sits back down, and reaches for his beer.

BILL

Emily all of a sudden wants me to tell her the future.

MICHAEL

Emily's a pretty remarkable girl.

BILL

Yeah, but Margaret's always fascinated me too.

MICHAEL

I'd go for the sure thing.

BILL

You would, huh?

MICHAEL

Emily loves you, you love her.

BILL

Yeah, but she's going away to France for three months.

MICHAEL

Well, don't you trust her?

BILL

Yeah, but I'm already the guy she's seeing behind her boyfriend's
back.

MICHAEL

That's complicated. But then Margaret's married to Walter.

BILL

But she just left him.

MICHAEL

That's true.

BILL

They could get back together, though.

MICHAEL

Happens all the time.

BILL

Unless I get in there now and make my play.

MICHAEL

Might be your only chance to know for sure.

Bill looks around, anxious and preoccupied.

INT. KITCHEN. MOMENTS LATER

*Trish is one of the waitresses. She's impatient, but Bill demands a
moment of her time.*

13

TRISH

Look, Bill, Margaret's in a very mixed-up place in her life right now. She doesn't need to get mixed up with someone like you.

BILL

Someone like me. What's that supposed to mean?

TRISH

You know what I mean.

BILL

No, I don't.

TRISH

You're not *serious*.

BILL

Serious like Walter, you mean?

TRISH

Hey! Walter's a pretty successful and well-thought-of guy most of the time!

BILL

He's smothering her.

TRISH

Well, that's no reason for her to take up with an aimless flirt like you.

BILL

Hey!

TRISH

You are with a different girl every time I see you!

BILL

So, I'm lucky!

TRISH

You're not lucky, Bill. You're loose.

He looks at her, lost. She explains.

You just can't career around from one cute little behind to the next, never investing anything in any one of them.

This stuns him a little, but he collects himself and comes right back at her.

BILL

What about Emily?

TRISH

What about Emily?

BILL

I've been with Emily for six months and I haven't strayed once!

TRISH

So, what do you want, a medal!

She walks away, angry and frustrated. He thinks about what she has said, then follows her. He gives his cigarettes to the Dishwasher, who is standing there overhearing all this.

BILL
(*to Dishwasher*)

Here. Go smoke my cigarettes.

The Dishwasher takes them and leaves.

(*to Trish*)

What? Are you upset?

TRISH

Your problems are trivial.

Nevertheless, she accepts him with relish as he leans down and kisses her on the mouth.

INT. MEN'S BATHROOM. MOMENTS LATER

Bill collapses in through the door and finds himself leaning over the sink. He sighs, then looks up at:

A group of men: Man #1 is washing his hands. Man #2 is at the urinal taking a leak. And Man #3 pauses as he steps out from one of the toilet stalls.

Bill looks down from them and gathers his wits. He speaks, still kneeling.

Gentlemen . . .
Excuse me.

They wait. He stands.

My girlfriend of *six* months is going away to Paris, France, for *three* months.

A discouraging collective sigh as they relax and settle. Bill moves to the urinals and takes a piss.

She's beautiful, young, intelligent and very conscientious. She says she loves me and that she'll miss me terribly.

She's also got this ex-boyfriend in Paris. He's real smart, talented, successful and he's a real nice guy.

Before she leaves, she wants me to tell her if there's a future for us. Me and her.

He steps away from the urinal and washes his hands.

My question is: am I wrong in wanting more time? More proof. Is it wrong of me to be so scared?

He steps away from the sink and waits for a reply.

MAN #1
It's important to keep the girl constantly within your sphere of influence. Of course, this is difficult to do if she is in another country. I would not feel guilty about this fear of losing her. People are people and things happen. But perhaps the things that do happen are not serious. I would write many letters. Daily if possible. And I do not think it inadvisable to let her know, frankly and before she leaves, that you have these fears of losing her. She's young. Perhaps she's impressionable. This sounds harsh and manipulating, I know, but remember, she's not just going anywhere; she's going to Paris, France.

MAN #2
Relinquishing our hold on someone is an act of love. The giving of affection and the determination to provide comfort are the two practicable elements of love.

Love requires no proof. Seen in this light, love is a sort of faith, since a faith that required proof wouldn't be a faith at all.

But I will make this distinction: love is an act and faith is an ability.

MAN #3

The best of all possible approaches to this dilemma is for the two of you to firmly embrace reality for what it is: cruel, brutal, cold, and totally unconcerned with the individual.

MAN #2

I don't want to sound despairing or at a loss for ideas, but the fact is you can do nothing to retain this girl's love but be the best man you know how to be.

INT. PUFFY'S TAVERN. MOMENTS LATER

Walter comes into the bar; he has a chip on his shoulder. He stands there looking around the place. Walter comes in and stands at the bar.

Mac and Michael and some other Guys hush themselves and watch him.

MAC

Hey, Walter.

WALTER

Bill been in here tonight?

MAC

He's in the men's room.

Walter places a handgun and a box of bullets on the bar as he reaches for his wallet.

WALTER

Gimme a bottle of Jack Daniels and two glasses, Mac. Thank you.

Mac does as he's told. Walter tosses two twenties on the bar and heads back to the tables.

Michael, Mac and the other Guys watch him go.

Bill comes out of the men's room and finds Walter sitting at a table, loading a gun.

Bill flashes a look over to . . .

Mac, Michael and the Guys just sit there, watching nervously. Mac starts to go for the phone, but . . .

Bill gestures for him to relax. He looks back over at Walter, pulls himself up, and approaches.

BILL

Evening, Walter.

Walter looks up, distraught, and finishes putting a single bullet in the gun. He lays the gun on the table and reaches for his drink.

WALTER

How are you, Bill?

BILL

Mind if I sit down?

WALTER
(self-pitying)

No. Why should *I* mind?

Bill sits down.

BILL
(of gun)

What are you gonna do with that?

WALTER

I'm gonna shoot myself.

BILL
(unloading gun)

That's pretty stupid, Walter.

WALTER

Yeah. I guess I oughta shoot Margaret, huh?

Bill pockets the bullet and lays the gun back down.

BILL
(pours a drink)

No. You're not gonna shoot anyone.

WALTER

Maybe I oughta shoot you.

19

BILL

Why me?

WALTER

Because you're a single guy with no responsibilities.

Bill looks away, unable to console the man.

Why is she doing this to me?

BILL

I don't know, Walter.

Walter takes up the gun and reloads it from a supply of bullets in his coat pocket. He puts just one in and lays the gun back down.

WALTER

She loved me once. Why can't she love me now?

BILL

People change.

WALTER

I don't change. I don't want to change.

BILL

Sometimes you have no choice.

WALTER

Have you changed?

Walter reaches over and calmly picks up the gun. He starts putting another bullet in.

BILL

I'm changing all the time.

WALTER

That's why the girls like you so much.

BILL

The girls don't all like me that much.

WALTER

Margaret likes you.

                    BILL
                (*intrigued*)
Did she say that?

   This confirms everything for Walter. He glares at Bill. Bill realizes it
   was a stupid thing to ask and leans back in his chair.

                    BILL
Look, Walter, nothing happened with Margaret and me.

                  WALTER
But it might.

                    BILL
Impossible.

                  WALTER
Why, don't you think she's attractive?

                    BILL
She's very attractive.

                  WALTER
She's my wife, goddamn it!
                (*silence, then*)
Why is it impossible? Why's nothing gonna happen between you
and Margaret?

                    BILL
                (*resigned*)
Because I'm in love with Emily.

                  WALTER
Liar.

                    BILL
                (*hurt*)
What?

                  WALTER
You've never loved anybody in your life. You go through women
like pairs of dirty underwear. You wouldn't know what
commitment was if it came up and bit you on the leg!

BILL
(*getting up*)
I don't have to sit here and listen to this.

WALTER
Yes, you do.

BILL
I gotta take Emily to the airport.

WALTER
Have a drink.

Bill acquiesces and sits back down.

They drink. Silence. Finally:

You ever think of settling down, Bill?

BILL
Occasionally.

WALTER
Lately?

BILL
A little.

WALTER
With Emily?

BILL
Probably.

WALTER
She's a good woman.

Bill considers this and slowly becomes convinced. He nods and sighs, resigned.

BILL
Yes, she is.

WALTER
You oughta propose to her.

BILL

You think so?

WALTER

Yeh.

Bill thinks about this, tosses the idea around, then:

BILL

Yeh, I guess you're right.

WALTER

You oughta do it now.

BILL

Excuse me?

Walter points the newly loaded gun at his head.

WALTER

Call her on the phone. Come on.

Walter leads him to the phone booth and hands him a quarter.

Bill stares at it, then up at Walter.

Walter shoves him into the booth.

Dial.

Bill just looks at him in shock.

Walter is blankly determined.

Bill swallows, scared, and looks out at . . .

Michael, Mac and Guys. They all just look on, frightened, but intrigued.

BILL

Will somebody do something? He's gotta gun, for crying out loud!

WALTER

Don't anyone move! I'll shoot 'im. I swear to God! I'll shoot 'im.

Walter jabs the gun up into Bill's back, but pauses and glares back over his shoulder at the bar.

No one moves.

Walter looks back at Bill.

Dial.

Bill hesitates, looks at the phone, hesitates some more, then sighs and dials.

Walter watches as . . .

Bill waits. But . . .

BILL

It's busy.

Walter, suspicious, grabs the receiver and listens.

WALTER
(*hanging up*)

Damn it!

They're just about to step from the booth, when . . .

RING ! ! ! ! ! ! !

They stop dead. Bill looks at Walter.

Walter looks from Bill to the phone.

Answer it.

Bill reaches out slowly and lifts the receiver.

BILL

Hello?

His face goes blank. Carefully, he looks out at Walter . . .

It's Margaret.

Walter steps back, confused and uncertain.

Bill returns to the phone, anxious to get her talking to Walter.

What? No. No. Don't worry about that. No. Really. Walter's here. You wanna talk to him?

Walter stands there anxiously, hopefully, pathetically.

24

Bill's face drops and he glances out at Walter.

(into phone)

No?

Walter's shoulders fall forward and he begins to dissolve.

Bill hangs up the phone, sadly. He looks out at Walter, commiserating.

Walter lowers the gun and holds it flat against his chest, staring at the floor.

Bill comes out to him and lays a hand on his shoulder. Walter, surprisingly, comes forward and presses himself against Bill, crying.

Bill tenses up at first and looks over at . . .

The Guys at the bar, who all look away in embarrassment.

But Bill returns his attention to Walter and hugs him. He holds him for a moment, then:

POW!!!!! The gun goes off and Bill falls back, holding his face.

OWWW!!!!!!

Bill falls back through some tables as . . .

Walter drops the gun, stunned.

Mac, Michael and the Guys rush over from the bar and help Bill up.

Bill rolls around on the floor, holding his face, bleeding a lot.

Walter collapses in a chair.

Michael leans down over him and looks. Going white, he gets back up and turns to Mac.

MICHAEL

He shot him in the face.

MAC

Get your truck! Quick! We gotta get him to a hospital!

Walter stands and tries to say something meaningful.

Mac shoves him back down in his seat, before returning to Bill.

The other Guys help Mac carry Bill out of the bar as Michael screeches to a halt out front in his truck.

Walter sits there shaking his head, destroyed.

INT. OPERATING ROOM. NIGHT

Doctor Clint, a female surgeon, is over Bill, who lies on the table. The Nurse is holding his head still as Clint inspects the wounds.

> CLINT

Hm-mm. This is bad.
> (*to Nurse*)

Can you wipe all this away.

The Nurse cleans up a portion of Bill's face as Clint steps aside to check her instruments. She moves back to Bill, down to business.

Now, we're going to have to give you something for the pain, but this is going to be painful in any event.

Bill nods.

Are you allergic to Novocaine?

> BILL

No.

She approaches with the needle, trying to decide how to proceed.

> CLINT

OK. Your entire upper lip is in three pieces. Can you feel that?

> BILL
> (*uncertain*)

I think so.

> CLINT

There are two tears. One goes right across the left cheek. You can feel that, can't you?

> BILL

Yes.

                           CLINT
Are you having any trouble breathing?

                           BILL
No.

                           CLINT
Good. Now I'm going to have to inject the Novocaine directly into
the wounds.

                           BILL
OK.

                           CLINT
I'm telling you this because it won't help to ignore what's going on
here. I'm going to need you to cooperate.

                           BILL
Right.

   Bill is scared. He stares straight up into the lights.

   Clint begins.

                           CLINT
This is going to pinch a little. There'll be a number of injections.

   *She makes the first injection and Bill stiffens and moans. Clint nods
   as she continues.*

I know. Uh-huh. I know.

   And she makes the next one.

                           NURSE
                        (*in his ear*)
Breathe.

                           CLINT
One more on this side.

   And he stiffens again.

                           NURSE
Just remember to breathe.

CLINT

This isn't going to last too long. It's running right out of you. There's no place for the Novocaine to stay. That's what's in your mouth right now. Novocaine. It's not blood. Do you need to spit?

The Nurse presses a wad of gauze up to the side of his face. He turns and drools into it.

NURSE

Keep thinking about something. Something specific.

BILL

I'm trying.

NURSE

What are you thinking about?

BILL

Girls.

NURSE

That's good. Tell me about the girls.

BILL

Soft skin. My hand cupping her breast. Caressing her bottom. Her thighs squeezing my leg. Kissing. Her tongue in my mouth. My mouth on her breast. Spooning.

NURSE
(dreamy and aroused)

Spooning?

BILL

We lie side by side . . . Your back to me . . . I put my arm around your waist . . . We draw up our knees.

The Nurse looks up and sees Doctor Clint watching her and Bill. She snaps out of it and . . .

NURSE

Keep still.

INT. HOSPITAL HALLWAY. AN HOUR LATER

*Bill comes out all bandaged up and puts on his coat. No one is there to
meet him. He sighs and looks at the floor.*

EXT. PHONE BOOTH. NIGHT

*Bill is listening on an outdoor pay phone as the number he has dialed
just rings and rings and rings. Finally, he hangs up and stands there in
the cold. Alone.*

EXT. STREETS. NIGHT

*Bill comes running across Lower Broadway hailing a taxi cab.
Reaching it, he throws open the door and calls in to the Driver.*

> BILL

Hey.

> DRIVER

What happened to you?

> BILL

I was shot by the husband of a woman I thought I might be in love
with. Can you take me to a bank machine and then out to the
airport?

> DRIVER

You gonna travel looking like that?

> BILL

What's wrong with the way I look?

> DRIVER

You got blood on your shirt.

But Bill's already in the car.

> BILL

Come on, let's go.

> DRIVER
> (*takes off*)

Where to?

Paris!

CUT TO BLACK

TITLE CARD: BERLIN OCTOBER 1944

[NOTE: Dialogue is in English, except where indicated otherwise.]

JOHAN
(*off, in German*)

I feel disgusting.

DWIGHT
(*off*)

What?

INT. JOHAN'S BERLIN APARTMENT. LATE AFTERNOON

Dwight is a young black American man, an out-of-work fashion model, lounging around on the couch, flipping through magazines and listening to loud music in the large, airy, and tastefully decorated apartment. He looks up only when the music is turned off.

JOHAN

He writes to me and says he misses me.
He calls and says he loves me. And I reply, 'I miss you too.' But I don't.

DWIGHT

Maybe you don't know what you feel.

Johan gets up from his desk, annoyed, and walks over to Dwight, demanding his attention.

JOHAN

But I *do* know what I feel.

Later. Dwight is now flipping through another magazine. Music is playing on the sound system again.

DWIGHT
(*calls*)

What time is your flight?

JOHAN
(*in the next room*)

Seven o'clock.

DWIGHT

Is he going to meet you at the airport in New York?

JOHAN

Yes.

DWIGHT

What are you gonna tell him?

Johan stops in the doorway.

JOHAN

What do you want me to tell him?

DWIGHT
(*wanders away*)

I don't want to tell you what to do.

JOHAN

Then tell me what you want.

DWIGHT

That would be the same thing.

JOHAN

It would help me decide.

DWIGHT

He wants you to stay with him in New York?

JOHAN
(*sighs*)

Yes.

SAME PLACE. LATER

Dwight barges into another room.

DWIGHT

What do you want me to say?

JOHAN

I want you to tell me if there is a future for me and you.

DWIGHT

A future, huh?

JOHAN

Yes.

Johan turns off the music.

DWIGHT

How can I answer that?

JOHAN
(*in German*)

Yes or no.

DWIGHT

I can't see the future.

Johan walks to the window and looks out at the street.

JOHAN

You don't need to see it if you know it's there.

SAME PLACE. LATER

Dwight throws on his new coat. It still has a price tag on it and Dwight tears it off. He takes one last glance at himself in the mirror, then crosses the room to Johan.

DWIGHT

Look, let me go get a car. I'll drive you out to the airport.

JOHAN

I can take a taxi.

DWIGHT

No! I want to. Can you wait here?

JOHAN

How long?

DWIGHT
(checks his watch)

An hour and a half.

JOHAN

Then what?

DWIGHT

Then I'll tell you the future.

JOHAN

At five-thirty?

DWIGHT

Without fail.

Johan considers this.

Dwight seems in earnest.

Finally . . .

JOHAN
(agrees)

Five-thirty.

Satisfied, Dwight jumps up, kisses Johan on the mouth, and flies out of the apartment.

EXT. JOHAN'S BUILDING. MOMENTS LATER

Dwight steps out onto the sidewalk, admires his new coat, and walks away.

EXT. STREET. MOMENTS LATER

Dwight strides happily along, full of anticipation.

EXT. TRAIN STATION. MOMENTS LATER

Dwight approaches a phone booth outside the station. As he nears it, though, a raunchy Prostitute races to beat him to it. The phone in the booth is off the hook.

She gets there and shoves Dwight out of the way with a crooked, confused, and good-natured smile. Lifting the receiver, she resumes her phone call.

WOMAN
(into phone, in German)

No.
No.
No.
No?

Indignant, Dwight wanders around to see if there is another phone booth. He doesn't see one. He wanders back, anxious. But the Woman is still going on.

(in German)

No.
No.

She and Dwight make eye contact. She smiles flirtatiously. Dwight moves off and waits to cross the street.

(in German)

No!
No.
No?
I've run out of money, I'll call you back in a minute.

34

She hangs up. Dwight rushes in, but she doesn't move. She turns and smiles at him.

> (*to Dwight, in German*)

My telephone card ran out. Can I use yours for a minute?

Dwight doesn't understand her. He just shrugs and looks lost. She realizes, then:

> (*in English*)

Can I use your phone card for just a minute?

Dwight hesitates, uncertain. She snatches it out of his hand and returns to the phone, dialing.

> WOMAN

I won't be long.

> DWIGHT
> (*angry*)

Fine.

He storms off.

> WOMAN
> (*into phone, in German*)

It's me again . . .
No . . .
No?

Dwight changes his mind after ten or so steps and comes right back to confront her.

> (*in German*)

No.
No.
No.
No.

Dwight throws open the door of the booth, but she just glances at him, unimpressed. She finishes up.

> (*in German*)

No.

No.
OK.
No.
Bye.

And she hangs up. Dwight puts his hand out for his phone card. She hands it to him.

WOMAN
(*in English*)

Sorry.

DWIGHT
(*curt*)

Don't worry about it.

WOMAN

Thank you.

DWIGHT

Yeah, right. See you around.

As she passes by him she grabs his crotch. Dwight freezes.

WOMAN

Maybe.

She stares him down a moment, then releases him and moves off.

Dwight watches her go, shocked. Finally, he puts his card back in and dials. He waits a moment, catching his breath, then:

DWIGHT
(*into phone*)

Werner?
It's me, Dwight.
It's important.
I need to ask you one question.
I want you to tell me if there's a future for me and you.
Yes or no.
You don't need to see it if you know it's there.
Meet me at the bar
    in ten minutes.

INT. CAFÉ. MOMENTS LATER

Dwight enters and the bartender screams at him immediately.

> MAC
> (*in German*)

You owe me money! ! ! !

> DWIGHT

Werner been in?

> MAC
> (*in German*)

You owe me money! ! ! !

> *Mac shakes his head and moves off.*

> *Dwight looks over to his friend, Elisabeth. She has a group of three men around her, all striking cool, disinterested poses. They regard Dwight with thinly veiled contempt as one of them recites from a book.*

> HARRY
> (*in German*)

Germans regard love as a virtue, a divine emanation, something mystical. It is not eager, impetuous, jealous and tyrannical, as it is in the heart of an Italian woman. It is deep, visionary, and utterly unlike anything in England.

> *Silence for a moment as Harry closes the book and smokes. Dick and Tom nod approvingly and sip their drinks.*

> *Dwight barges into the middle of all this and sits down. Tom gets up in a huff and leaves.*

> DWIGHT

Elisabeth, can I borrow your car? I've got to get Johan out to the airport.

> TOM

Hasn't he thrown you out yet?

> *Dwight flashes him a look.*

DWIGHT

He's just going away to New York because he's got some work to do there for three months.

But Harry is not convinced. Dwight looks from him to Dick, who looks away and sips his drink.

DICK

Did you hear the news?

HARRY
(*as if on cue*)

What news?

DICK
(*significantly*)

Werner left Greta.

Everyone gasps. Dwight looks from one to the other, then:

TOM

Do you know that for a fact?

Dick and Harry refuse to say more. Dick gets up and sashays away.

Dwight looks to Elisabeth.

39

ELISABETH
(*with authority*)

I heard it from Simone.

Dwight pauses, then sits back, thinking.

Elisabeth looks on, amused.

Harry lingers nearby, eager for gossip.

DWIGHT
(*to Elisabeth*)

Something happened between Werner and me.

ELISABETH

Oh yeah, like what?

DWIGHT

We got romantic.

ELISABETH

Excuse me?

DWIGHT

Romantic.

Elisabeth looks to Harry.

HARRY
(*in German*)

Romantic?

DWIGHT

We kissed.

They both turn and look at him.

Once.

ELISABETH

When?

DWIGHT

A few weeks ago.

HARRY

How?

Dwight pauses, thinks, then gets up and kisses Harry ferociously on the mouth. Elisabeth looks on as he steps back again and Harry, breathlessly indignant, tries to slap him. But Dwight stays his hand, twists his arm, and shoves him away from the table.

EXT. STREET. MOMENTS LATER

Dwight and Elisabeth are approaching her car. Elisabeth seems eager to usher this scandal into existence.

ELISABETH

But what about Johan?

DWIGHT

Johan all of a sudden wants me to tell him the future.

ELISABETH

Johan's a remarkable man.

DWIGHT

Yeah, but Werner's always fascinated me too.

They reach the car and she hands him the keys.

ELISABETH

I'd go for the sure thing.

DWIGHT

You would, huh?

ELISABETH

Johan loves you.

She watches Dwight struggle with this little truth, then:

And you love him.

DWIGHT

But he's going away to America for three months.

ELISABETH

Well, don't you trust him?

DWIGHT

I'm already the guy he's seeing behind his boyfriend's back.

ELISABETH

That is complicated. But then Werner's married to Greta.

DWIGHT
(*accusing*)

But he just left her!

ELISABETH

That's true.

DWIGHT

But they could get back together again.

ELISABETH

Happens all the time.

DWIGHT

Unless I get in there now and make my play.

ELISABETH

It might be your only chance to know it for sure.

He starts the car and drives off. Elisabeth watches him go, grinning.

INT. POSTMUSEUM. DAY

A nude female Model stands waiting in the cavernous old landmark building. Simon(e), an effeminate gay man and fashion stylist, approaches and begins helping her into an outfit. Dwight wanders around, looking at the building.

> SIMON(E)
> Dwight, Werner is at a really complicated place in his life right now. He doesn't need to be getting mixed up with someone like you.

> DWIGHT
> Someone like me. What's that supposed to mean?

> SIMON(E)
> You know what I mean.

> DWIGHT
> No, I don't. What do you mean?

Simon(e) spins the Model around, checks the clothes, and leads her off to the photo shoot.

> SIMON(E)
> You're not serious.

> DWIGHT
> Serious like his wife, you mean?

> SIMON(E)
> Greta is a pretty successful and well-thought-of woman most of the time.

> DWIGHT
> She's smothering him.

> SIMON(E)
> Well, that's no reason for him to take up with an aimless flirt like you.

> DWIGHT
> Hey!

SIMON(E)
You are with a different man every time I see you.

DWIGHT
So, I'm lucky.

SIMON(E)
(*in German*)
You're not lucky. You're loose.

DWIGHT
(*in German*)
Loose?

SIMON(E)
(*in German*)
Loose.

Dwight steps away and searches for 'Schlampe' *in his German/ English dictionary.*

SAME PLACE. LATER

The photo shoot is moving. Dwight and Simon(e) walk along with the Model, the Photographer, and her Assistant.

DWIGHT

What about Johan?

SIMON(E)

What about Johan?

DWIGHT

I've been with Johan for six months and I haven't strayed once.

Simon(e) loses his patience and stops, screaming.

SIMON(E)

So what do you want me to do, give you a medal!

Dwight is shocked. He calls after Simon(e) as he walks away.

DWIGHT

Are you upset?

Simon(e) comes back and circles around him, seething.

SIMON(E)

Your problems are trivial.

The whole crowd marches off and Dwight is left alone. He takes out a cigarette and lights up. After a moment's thought he addresses three Laborers who have been doing restoration work on the old building and have overheard this whole conversation.

DWIGHT

There's this man, right. Johan. He's great. We have been together for like six months. But now he's got to go to New York for like three months and work.

He's handsome. He's, you know . . . older. He's extremely intelligent and he's got excellent taste. He works very hard.

He says he loves me. Says he'll miss me, sure, but look, he's got this like totally excellent ex-boyfriend back there in New York; smart, good-looking, successful . . . and of course he's a really nice guy too.

Now before Johan leaves Berlin – in an hour – he wants me to tell him if there's a future us; for me and him.

My question is this: am I wrong to want more time? More proof. Is it wrong of me to be scared?

45

He looks at them, pauses, waits for a response, then remembers the time. He checks his watch, throws away his cigarettes, and takes off.

The three Laborers watch him go and it appears they have not understood a word he has said. Then, in German:

BORIS

I think he's wrong.

PETER

You do?

BORIS

I don't know why he's scared. I think he wants too much for too little.

MIKE

I think he has a legitimate reason for hesitating. Besides his own indecision, this man, Johan, has in fact shown himself to be capable of infidelity; he's cheating on his lover in New York.

PETER

But then we don't know if Johan ever displayed the same urge to commit to this other man in New York the way he has with Dwight.

BORIS
(impatient)

The point is, Dwight's been given an ultimatum. He should know how he feels. He's acting in bad faith. He wants the situation to remain ambiguous indefinitely.

PETER

He's a flirt.

BORIS

Exactly.

MIKE

To flirt is to exist in ambiguity. Flirtation denotes nothing more and nothing less than chaste amorous relations generally devoid of deep feelings. Yes, Dwight, like Bill in New York City, is a flirt. For people like this to define what the situation really is between

46

themselves and . . . well, the other . . . this is to destroy the very possibility of flirtation . . .

> BORIS

So what? Are you standing up for him?

> MIKE

For who?

> BORIS

For Dwight.

> MIKE

No. But I think Johan's ultimatum is a little exaggerated.

> PETER
> (*agrees with Mike*)

Perhaps Johan is quite fond of Dwight's flirtatiousness.

> BORIS

But this isn't about flirtation. It's about seduction.

> PETER

It's just a matter of degree.

> BORIS

He's trying to steal some woman's husband.

> PETER

Ah, he's just having some fun.

> MIKE

You know to seduce is, etymologically, to 'lead astray', to make someone take the wrong turn.

> BORIS

You see, that sounds more like what's going on here.

> PETER

Look, we don't know for sure if Werner's leaving his wife because Dwight kissed him.

> BORIS

If we can believe what he tells us, the film-maker's project here has been to compare the changing dynamics of one situation in different milieus.

                              MIKE
And you don't think he'll succeed?

                              BORIS
Well, it's too early to tell, perhaps. But no, I think he will fail.

                              PETER
                     (*enthusiastically*)
Yes, he'll fail. He already has failed. But in this case the failure is interesting.

                              BORIS
                     (*he has had enough*)
Why don't you just shut the fuck up!

                              PETER
The milieu is bound to change the dynamics of the situation.

                              BORIS
People are the same no matter what the milieu is.

                              MIKE
So, you don't think personality, character, has any effect on situation?

                              BORIS
Stop twisting my words around.

                              PETER
The question, though, remains the same. What do you do when contingent reality demands definitive response?

                              BORIS
We cannot exist in ambiguity for ever!

                              MIKE
I disagree. I think we can. Although I think it would be the deepest kind of isolation.

EXT. COURTYARD. DAY

Dwight pulls up in the car and approaches Werner's house. He enters

the courtyard. There is a little girl who stops playing and looks at him. She watches as he comes in and approaches one of the doors leading up to the apartments.

INT. WERNER'S APARTMENT. DAY

Coming carefully into the apartment, Dwight finds . . .

Greta, Werner's distraught wife, pacing forlornly in the kitchen. She's a wreck and the place is a mess. It's also a home of moderate poverty. We can see the signs of Werner's painting activity: stretched canvases stacked against walls, work tables covered with paint, etc.

Dwight stops in the doorway, but it's too late.

Greta stops when she sees him. She stares at him.

Dwight dares not move.

Greta pauses a moment more, then, taking a step forward, utters:

> GRETA
> (*in German*)

Why is he doing this to me?

Dwight has no idea what she's talking about. He turns to leave. But he stops when he sees . . .

The little girl, Greta's daughter, standing between him and the door, blocking his way.

He turns back to Greta and finds her right there in front of him.

He loved me once. Why can't he love me now?

DWIGHT

People change.

GRETA

I don't change.

DWIGHT

Maybe you will.

GRETA

I don't want to change!

And she takes her Daughter by the hand, sits her on a chair, and ties her shoelace. She sends her on her way, then sits in the chair herself, tired and weak.

DWIGHT
(*compassionately*)

Look, Greta, nothing happened between me and Werner.

GRETA

But it might.

DWIGHT

No, it won't.

Dwight falls on the bed and starts flipping through some magazines.

GRETA

Why isn't anything going to happen between you and Werner?

DWIGHT

I'm in love with Johan.

She thinks a moment, then mumbles:

GRETA
(*in German*)

Liar.

DWIGHT

What?

GRETA

Do you ever think of settling down, Dwight?

DWIGHT

Occasionally.

GRETA

Lately.

DWIGHT

A little.

GRETA

With Johan?

DWIGHT

Probably.

GRETA

He's a good man.

DWIGHT

Yes, he is.

GRETA

Call him on the phone.

Dwight does as he's told. He crosses to the table, sits, lifts the receiver, but hesitates.

Dial.

He dials. She comes and stands over him. He waits. Then:

DWIGHT

It's busy.

Greta grabs the phone and listens. She hears the busy signal and slams it down.

GRETA
(*in German*)

Damn!

She collapses into a chair.

The phone rings.

She glares at it.

Dwight looks on, careful. They look at each other a moment, then:

Answer it.

Dwight hesitates, scared, then picks up the receiver.

DWIGHT

Hello?
(*brightening up*)
Werner!
(*to Greta*)
It's Werner.
(*back to phone*)
What? No. No. Don't worry about that. No. Really. Greta's here.
You want to talk to her?

But he stops, pauses, hesitates.

No.

*And Werner hangs up. Dwight looks at the receiver in disbelief, then
over to Greta.*

Greta is furious.

*Dwight hangs up the phone and looks on compassionately as she
moves to the set of drawers by the bed.*

*He wishes he could say something comforting, but he can't. He sits at
the table and hangs his head, but looks up again and sees . . .*

Greta remove a gun from the top drawer.

He freezes.

She sits on the edge of the bed and holds the gun to her chest.

53

Now what are you gonna do with that?

GRETA

I'm gonna shoot myself.

DWIGHT

That's pretty stupid, Greta

GRETA

Yeah. I guess I ought to shoot Werner, huh?

He comes over and kneels before her.

DWIGHT

No. You're not gonna shoot anyone.

GRETA

Maybe I should shoot you.

Dwight looks back over his shoulder at . . .

Greta's Daughter standing in the doorway, looking on.

He looks back at . . .

The gun in Greta's hands, then up at her face turned away from him.

54

He stands and crosses to the little girl.

DWIGHT
(*off*)

Here, go smoke my cigarettes.

He comes back to the bed and stands before Greta. She looks him up and down, then grabs him by his belt buckle and swings him down on to the bed.

He doesn't know what to do.

She lays her head on his shoulder and he goes rigid, scared. But he keeps calm and, slowly, places his arm around the distraught woman while holding fast to the bedstead with his free hand.

Greta receives this tentative embrace like a thirsty person being given a glass of water and she swings her arm up around his neck, desperate for the consolation of even a disinterested hug.

Dwight holds his breath and rolls his eyes to the ceiling as Greta curls up against him like a child, although she still has the gun clutched tightly in her hand.

Dwight braces himself for the unthinkable, releases his sweaty grip on the bedstead, passes his arm around her waist, and lowers Greta to the mattress.

Her Daughter gets up from where she has been spying by the door and walks back outside to play.

Dwight, meanwhile, kisses Greta on the mouth while he tries to remove the gun from her hand.

EXT. COURTYARD/WERNER'S. SAME TIME

Greta's Daughter plays in the courtyard as her father, Werner, arrives drunk and staggering.

He picks her up, hugs her, and kisses her on the cheek. Putting her back down, he stumbles on into the house. The Daughter continues playing while we hear the sound of a distant commotion upstairs.

Boom! A gunshot.

55

The little girl nearly jumps out of her skin, freezes, and stares at the house.

A Neighbour comes our from across the courtyard, concerned but uncertain. Greta then comes running out of the house, half dressed and horrified. She picks up her Daughter and backs away across the courtyard.

Dwight now stumbles out and the Neighbour screams. Greta throws herself back against the building as Dwight trips and falls, his face all bloody.

She runs to her Daughter and picks her up in her arms. Then Werner stumbles out, drunk and overwhelmed. They all look on as . . .

Dwight staggers to the road and falls against Elisabeth's car.

INT. HOSPITAL OPERATING ROOM. DAY

The Doctor is over Dwight, who lies on the table. The Nurse is busy preparing as the Doctor inspects the wounds.

> DOCTOR
> (*in German*)

This looks bad.

> (*to Nurse*)

Could you clean this, please?

The Nurse begins cleaning a part of Dwight's face.

I'm going to give you something for the pain, but it's still going to hurt.

> DWIGHT

What?

> DOCTOR
> (*in German*)

Are you allergic to Novocaine?

> DWIGHT

What's he saying?

> NURSE

Are you allergic to Novocaine?

No.

NURSE
(*to Doctor*)

No.

DOCTOR
(*in German*)

Your upper lip is in three pieces. Can you feel that?

NURSE

Can you feel that?

DWIGHT

Feel what!

DOCTOR
(*in German*)

You have two tears. One goes right up the side of your nose.

NURSE

There are two tears. One goes right up the side of your nose.

DWIGHT

Oh man!

DOCTOR
(*to Nurse, in German*)

Can he feel that?

DWIGHT

Yes!

The Nurse nods to the Doctor, who is waiting for translation.
Satisfied, he lays a hand on Dwight's shoulder and asks, in English:

DOCTOR

Are you having any trouble breathing?

DWIGHT

No.

DOCTOR

Good.

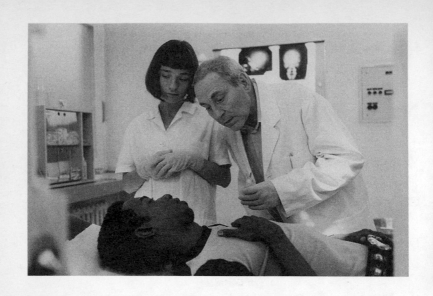

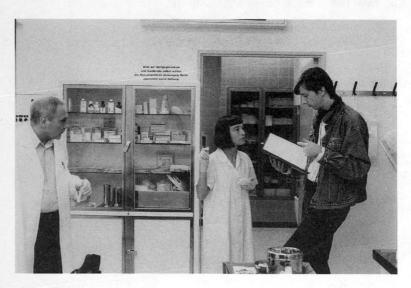

(then, in German)
Now I have to inject the Novocaine straight into the wound. OK?

DWIGHT
(lost)
OK.

DOCTOR
(in German)
I'm telling you this because it won't help if you don't know what's going on. I will need your help.

DWIGHT
What's he saying?

NURSE
Keep still.

DOCTOR
(in German)
It's going to sting a bit. A few more shots.

He makes the first of these injections and Dwight stiffens into an arc.

I know . . . Hm-mm. I know . . .

NURSE
Breathe.

DOCTOR
(in German)
Good. Now on this side . . .

Dwight reacts again.

NURSE
Just remember to breathe.

DOCTOR
(concerned, in German)
It won't hold for very long. It's running straight back out again.
The Novocaine doesn't have anywhere to go.
(to Dwight)
Do you need to spit?

The Nurse presses a wad of gauze up to the side of his face and has Dwight drool into it as . . .

NURSE

Keep thinking about something. Something specific.

DWIGHT

I'm trying.

NURSE

Good. What are you thinking about?

DWIGHT

Guys.

NURSE

That's good. Tell me about the guys.

DWIGHT

Muscles.
My hand on his ass.
My cock in his hand.

The Doctor pauses and looks on, confused.

Kissing
His tongue in my mouth.
My mouth on his chest.
Spooning.

DOCTOR
(*to Nurse, intrigued*)

'Spooning'?

But the Nurse is busy trying to calm Dwight down. She doesn't answer. The Doctor then lifts the sharp, shiny instruments used for stitching and approaches the operating table.

DWIGHT
(*continues*)

We lay side by side.
Your back to me.
I put my arm around your waist.
We draw up our knees.

(*in German*)

What's he talking about?

*The Nurse looks at the Doctor, decides not to answer him, then
returns to Dwight.*

NURSE
(*to Dwight*)

Keep still.

EXT. BUILDING ENTRANCE. NIGHT

*Dwight is buzzing Johan's apartment, but there is no answer. He steps
out into the street and looks up to the dark apartment, then returns and
keeps buzzing anyway. He stops, frustrated, and sees a homosexual
couple walk by, laughing.*

Finally, he gives up and walks away.

EXT. *IMBISS* (SNACK BAR). NIGHT

Dwight comes over to the Imbiss. *There is a man standing there,
having a beer. Dwight empties his pocket of a few small coins and lays
them on the counter. The woman behind the counter leans over, sees it is
not enough to buy anything, then pushes the pile back towards Dwight.
Dwight takes back his meager offering and walks to the far end of the
Imbiss. He leans back and hugs himself against the cool evening air.*

MAN
(*in German*)

What happened to you?

Dwight looks at him, pauses, then:

DWIGHT

I got shot by the wife of a man I thought I might be in love with.

The Man nods and drinks his beer.

Dwight shivers.

*The Man sees this and comes closer, removing his jacket and offering
it to Dwight. Dwight is charmed and takes the jacket. He leans*

against the Imbiss *and smiles, but smiling hurts his face.*

As the Man leans back and enjoys his beer, Dwight looks out at the night and sighs, sadly.

FADE TO BLACK.

TITLE CARD: TOKYO MARCH 1995

[NOTE: When the Japanese characters speak among themselves they use their own language. When they speak with Hal Hartley, they speak in English.]

INT. SCHOOL REHEARSAL HALL. DAY

Miho, Yuki and six Male Dancers are led through a rehearsal for a dance piece by their choreographer/director, Mr Ozu.

The movement revolves around the simple action of Miho approaching Yuki, who is curled up on the floor, and helping her to stand.

Ozu moves confidently among the dancers; directing them, sometimes stopping them and performing a gesture himself.

He works particularly closely with Miho, attenuating her gestures and conducting the rhythm of her movement.

Yuki watches this with resentment.

The short section of the piece is then executed by Miho and Yuki.

Then the next section is executed: the Male Dancers manipulate Miho so that she comes down over Yuki and embraces her. More Male Dancers move up and position Yuki's arms around Miho, so that they are embracing each other.

SAME PLACE. LATER

The rehearsal is over and everyone is getting ready to leave. Ozu sits, preoccupied, and reviews his notes. He is a handsome and dynamic man.

INT. HALLWAY/BATHROOM. TWENTY MINUTES LATER

Miho comes up the hall and stops when she hears someone crying in the bathroom. She approaches carefully. Looking in, she sees . . .

Ozu washing his hands at the sink while Yuki, his wife, crosses in front of him and holds a gun to her head. Unfazed, Ozu shakes off the water from his hands, grabs the gun, and checks to see if it's loaded. Yuki then jumps forward, grabs the gun back, and slaps him in the face.

Ozu now sees Miho. Yuki follows his gaze and sees her as well.

Yuki storms out, passes Miho, and runs away down the hall, where another Student is startled to see the gun. Yuki disappears down the hall and the Student runs past Miho, panicked.

Miho watches her go, but then looks back in at . . .

Ozu, as he comes out into the hall. He leans against the window and sighs wearily, deeply troubled.

Miho is concerned. She moves to a water cooler and gets him a drink. She brings it to him.

He sees the water, takes it, and drinks. He looks to Miho and laughs when she puts on her hat; it's an odd but pretty antique. She smiles as she shows it off. Ozu takes it from her head and studies it. Then he starts crying and hugs her to himself.

Miho is startled. But, finally, she gives in and hugs Ozu in return, trying to calm him down.

He appreciates this and his tears subside. He leans back away from her and looks her in the eye. She doesn't know what to say.

He leans forward to kiss her and she backs away. He hesitates, but then moves forward again and kisses her on the mouth. He leans back, watching her blank surprise, then sees someone down the hall. Miho follows his gaze to see . . .

Her friend Naomi and two other Dancers looking at them from the staircase. They all take off, scandalized.

Ozu snaps out of it. He pulls himself together and stands up straight. He smiles, suddenly filled with energy and confidence.

He caresses Miho's cheek, then bounds dynamically down the hall.

Miho stands there, confused, but pleasantly breathless.

INT. HALL. SOME TIME LATER

Miho comes dreamily out and walks down the hall. Naomi catches up and walks alongside.

NAOMI

Miho, Ozu-san is in a complicated place in his life right now. He doesn't need to be getting mixed up with someone like you.

MIHO
(*far away*)

Someone like me? What's that supposed to mean?

NAOMI

You know what I mean.

MIHO
(*stops*)

No, I don't.

NAOMI

You're not serious.

Miho considers this, then sits on a bench in the hall and takes off her hat.

MIHO

Serious like his wife, you mean?

NAOMI

Yuki is a pretty successful and well-thought-of woman most of the time.

MIHO

She's smothering him.

NAOMI

Well that's no reason for him to take up with an aimless flirt like you.

Miho looks up at her, hurt.

Naomi spins on her heel and leaves.

Miho looks off and sees . . .

A couple of Male Dancers are watching her.

EXT. STREET. DAY

Miho walks through a busy city street and stops before entering a particular building to apply lipstick. Satisfied with how she looks, she enters the building.

INT. EDIT ROOM. DAY

Hal is on the phone, pacing around the cutting room, while his assistant editor, Nagase, works at the rewinds.

HAL

No.
No.
No!
No.

> *Nagase looks up as Miho enters. He continues working as she puts down her things and Hal slams down the phone.*

HAL

I feel disgusting.

MIHO

Why?

> *Hal doesn't answer. He sits back down at the Steenbeck.*

What time is your flight?

HAL

Seven.

MIHO

Is she going to meet you at the airport in Los Angeles?

HAL

Yes.

> *Nagase keeps busy at the rewinds, listening.*

MIHO

What do you want me to say?

HAL

I want you to tell me if there is a future for us.

MIHO

How can I answer that?

67

HAL

Yes or no.

MIHO

I can't see the future.

Hal gets up, takes the script off a shelf, flips through it, and finds the line. He recites:

HAL
(*reading*)

'You don't need to see it if you know it's there.'

Miho comes over, takes the script away from him, and throws it in the garbage. Nagase looks on, concerned about the script.

MIHO

I'll go borrow Naomi's car and drive you out to the airport.

HAL

I can take a taxi.

MIHO

No. I want to. Can you wait here?

                              HAL

How long?

                              MIHO

An hour and a half.

                              HAL

And then what?

                              MIHO

Then I'll tell you the future.

                              HAL

In an hour and a half?

                              MIHO

I promise.

*He takes her wrist and looks at the time on a watch that is way too
big for her, a man's watch.*

                              HAL

At five-thirty?

                              MIHO

Without fail.

                              HAL

OK. Five-thirty.

They kiss.

*She leaves. Nagase watches her go. When the door is closed behind
her, he turns to Hal, who has resumed his search for trims.*

                             NAGASE

You owe me money, man.

                              HAL

I owe lots of people money.

EXT. ENTRANCE TO SAME BUILDING. MOMENTS LATER

Miho approaches a pay-phone, gets out her phone card, and dials.

Nagase passes by her and goes to the vending machines to get a few cans of beer. He overhears Miho on the pay-phone.

MIHO

Mr Ozu?
It's me, Miho . . .
I, uh . . .
Uh . . . have something important . . .
I just ne . . .
I just need to . . .
I just need to ask you . . .
Will you tell me if there is there a future for us?
Yes . . .
You don't need to see it, if it's there.
All right. I'll see you in ten minutes.

She hangs up and glances at Nagase before heading out into the street.

INT. SCHOOL. TEN MINUTES LATER

Miho enters and knocks on Ozu's office door. She calls to Naomi as she is passing by.

MIHO

Naomi, can I borrow your car? I have to drive Hal out to the airport.

NAOMI
(*cruelly*)

He's finally leaving you, huh?

Miho just looks at her, stunned. She waits a moment, then steps away and sits. Finally, she speaks, but without much confidence.

MIHO

He's just going to Los Angeles for three months . . . to do some work he has there.

Now Naomi feels bad. She looks at her hands and sighs. She comes over to Miho, hands her the car keys, and continues kindly.

                              NAOMI
Don't you trust him?

                              MIHO
I'm already the girl he's seeing behind his girlfriend's back.

*Naomi thinks this over then sits back, unable to say anything
optimistic. She gets up and leaves.*

Left alone, Miho looks up as she sees . . .

*Two Policemen, Tomo and Mochi, enter the school and climb up the
stairs beside her. The younger policeman, Tomo, watches her shyly.*

*She watches them disappear up on to the second floor, then turns
back and is startled to discover Yuki sitting right there next to her.*

                              YUKI
                          (*whispering*)
Why is he doing this to me?

                              MIHO
                          (*whispering*)
I don't know.

                              YUKI
He loved me once. Why can't he love me now?

                              MIHO
People change.

                              YUKI
I don't change.

                              MIHO
Maybe you will.

                              YUKI
I don't want to change.

                              MIHO
Sometimes you have no choice.

                              YUKI
Do you change?

                               71

                              MIHO
I'm changing all the time.

                              YUKI
That's why all the men like you so much.

                              MIHO
The men don't all like me that much.

                              YUKI
My husband likes you.

Miho just looks at her, terrified. Then they both look up when they hear . . .

Ozu striding up the hall.

He comes over to them and looks up the stairs where he hears the Policemen marching around. Then he looks at Yuki.

Miho looks on as Ozu and Yuki struggle for the gun.

Finally, he gets it from her and pauses to hear if the cops are approaching.

He grabs Miho's hat off her head again, shoves the gun inside, and gives it to Miho, pointing to the exit at the end of the hall. Miho is torn between doing what is asked of her and attending to Yuki, who is huddled up in the corner, sobbing.

But she obeys Ozu, who forcefully ushers her towards the door. He then mounts the stairs to deal with the cops.

Yuki comes forward and looks off at the exit Miho has passed through.

EXT. BACK OF BUILDING. MOMENTS LATER

Miho jumps out into the alley and the door swings shut behind her.

She looks around and tries to think. She wanders up the alley, looking for a place to dump the gun.

She finds a garbage can and dumps it in there. Walking on, she realizes she has thrown away her hat. She returns to get it from the garbage. As she does so, she sees an old Homeless Man digging through the garbage cans further on up the alley. She thinks a moment, then retrieves the gun and walks off to find another, safer, place to hide it.

She strolls up the alley, holding the gun out in full view. Rounding a corner into another alley she stops.

A Business Couple are standing there before her, petrified.

Miho is startled, too.

They look from her to the gun.

She realizes this and hides the gun behind her back, then turns and runs as . . .

The Couple look on in horror.

EXT. ANOTHER ALLEY. SAME TIME

Miho finds herself alone and looks around frantically for some place to ditch the gun. She spots . . .

A bicycle leaning up against the back of a yakatori *shop (eating place).*

She dumps the gun into the garbage in the basket on the bike's handlebars and runs up towards the far end of the alley.

But Yuki has followed her. She emerges from the shadows at the far end of the alley and descends upon the gun's hiding place.

EXT. STREET. SAME TIME

Miho walks out into the crowded streets and feels relieved. She checks her watch, sighs, and keeps moving.

INT. BOOKSHOP. SAME TIME

Miho enters and moves directly in among the shelves, trying to mix in with the crowd. She moves from section to section, flipping through books and magazines at random, always keeping an eye on the entrance to see if she has been followed.

One of the books she happens to pick up interests her and she reads quietly to herself as she strolls through the aisles . . .

'Love is an actual thing.
We ourselves bring it into existence.
These words, these written pages,
the melody of the sentences,
the images they conjure . . .
these are not just the products of love,
nor are they merely the expression of love . . .
they are a *form* love has taken.
They are *actually* my love.'

She looks up and sees . . .

People looking at her.

Embarrassed, she closes the book and steps down the aisle to continue browsing. But she sees another Young Couple fall back away from her with dread.

She looks around and sees . . .

The Business Couple pointing her out to the Policemen we saw earlier at the school, Tomo and Mochi. They rush in after her.

EXT. STREET. SAME TIME

They drag her down the street and into the alley where she hid the gun. A small crowd has followed.

She points to where she hid it and is held back by the older Policeman, Mochi, while the younger one, Tomo, goes and searches.

He finds nothing.

In disbelief, Miho runs forward and looks for herself. She finds nothing and falls back, afraid.

The small crowd looks on, shaking their heads in dismay.

EXT. STREET. MOMENTS LATER

Tomo and Mochi drag her up the street and throw her into a police car. She is driven off.

EXT. EDIT ROOM BUILDING. SAME TIME

Hal waits for Miho. Nagase is loading the trunk of a taxi cab with film cans.

NAGASE

Hal, come on! It's time to go!

HAL

Has Miho been in?

CAB DRIVER
(*in Japanese*)

You owe me money!

Hal just looks at him, perplexed. He puts change in the beer machine and gets two cans.

NAGASE

Hal, man, Miho is with a different guy every time I see her.

HAL

So, she's lucky.

NAGASE

She's not lucky, man. She's loose.

Hal can't really understand his English and asks . . .

HAL

'Loose'?

NAGASE

Loose.

Hal continues loading the film cans into the trunk.

HAL

What about me?

NAGASE

What about you?

HAL

I've been with Miho for, like, six months and she hasn't strayed once.

NAGASE
(*unimpressed*)

So what!

And he hands Hal the last film can. Hal puts it in the trunk, moves his two cans of beer from one pocket of his jacket to the other, then reaches in and pulls out a stack of yen, which he hands to Nagase.

As Hal closes the trunk and gets into the cab, Nagase counts his money.

INT. POLICE STATION. AN HOUR LATER

Miho, seated beside a desk in the busy station, is being tormented by Mochi, who is playing the 'bad cop', while Tomo, who will be playing the 'good cop', gets her a cup of water.

MOCHI
(*to Miho*)

What's the matter? Are you upset?

She nods 'yes'.

Your problems are trivial.

Tomo hands Miho the cup of water and she takes it gratefully. She is pretty shook up. She drinks slowly, pauses, then:

MIHO

Something happened between my teacher and me.

Yeah? Like what?

They wait as she thinks about how to say this. Then:

MIHO

We kissed. Once.

Tomo sits back, deeply disappointed in her. Mochi puts on his cap and marches out of the office.

INT. HOLDING CAGE. MOMENTS LATER

Miho is locked up with three other women.

They are an odd lot: a traditional Japanese married woman, a tense businesswoman, and a fierce young motorcycle chick.

They say nothing as she looks at them. Finally, she turns away and leans against the door.

MIHO

My boyfriend is from America and we have been together for six months. Now he is going away to Los Angeles for three months to work.

He says he loves me and that he will miss me very much.

But there is another woman in Los Angeles – his ex-girlfriend. She wants to marry him. She is very beautiful and successful and intelligent. She is a very nice person.

Before he leaves, he wants me to tell him if there is a future for us – for me and him.

(*turns back to the others*)

Am I wrong to hesitate? Is it wrong of me to want more time? More proof? Is it wrong of me to be so scared?

She waits. They say nothing. Then, all of a sudden, they all start speaking at once. The tough, younger, motorcycle chick, Kazuko:

KAZUKO

Fuck him! He's manipulating you! Who the hell does he think he is! A gift from God! Tell him to get lost! His leaving Japan is the best thing that ever happened to you! The fuck!

The fearful, desperate businesswoman, Shoko:

SHOKO

Don't let him go! He'll get away! You were wrong to want more time! A girl has to make a choice! You won't be young for ever! Western men are more open-minded! They like Asian women!

The kind, gentle, philosophical Narumi:

NARUMI

Nobody's perfect. We're all incomplete. We have to understand that the people we love have had lives before meeting us. They have histories. And their time with us is a separate history. No, nobody's perfect. We're all banged up and broken. It's embarrassing. Pathetic. Human.

Tomo arrives and bangs on the cage. They all shut up. He unlocks the cage and motions to Miho.

INT. POLICE STATION. MOMENTS LATER

Miho is given back her stuff. She puts the watch back on her wrist and checks the time. It's six o'clock.

She looks up, alarmed, and looks around for a phone.

80

INT. POLICE STATION/PHONE. MOMENTS LATER

She dials frantically. It rings. She waits for someone to pick it up.

INT. EDIT ROOM. SAME TIME

Nagase is still counting his money. The phone is ringing and he curses under his breath as he goes to answer it.

NAGASE

Yeah . . . No . . . He's gone.

He hangs up and continues counting his money.

INT. POLICE STATION. SAME TIME

Miho stands there, staring at the phone, depressed. She hangs up slowly, then wanders away towards the exit. But she looks up as . . .

Mochi enters the station with Ozu by the arm. Ozu, seeing Miho, takes a step towards her. But, Mochi grabs him and tosses him into a room off the hall.

Miho looks on as Tomo forces Ozu into a seat and slams the door.

She stands there in the hall, exhausted and confused.

EXT. POLICE STATION. SAME TIME

Miho comes out and stands there, wondering what to do. She reaches into her pocket and rediscovers Naomi's car keys. This gives her an idea.

She looks around and sees . . .

A bike leaning against the building. She runs to it, hops on, and takes off.

Tomo and Mochi are watching her from a distance. They hop in their squad car and follow.

Miho rides through town, weaving in and out of back alleys.

EXT. SCHOOL. NIGHT

Finally, she drops the bike outside the school and rushes to Naomi's car,

parked there in the street. But as she lifts the keys to the lock, she sees . . .

One of Hal's film cans lying on its side near the entrance of the school.

Miho drops the keys and moves to the can. After inspecting it, she looks up at the empty school and enters.

INT. SCHOOL. MOMENTS LATER

Miho comes in the front door and listens. There seems to be no one in the building. She continues further into the main hall.

She reaches the stairs and climbs to the second floor.

She reaches the second-floor landing and listens again. Finally, she comes up the hall and looks into the rehearsal studio. She sees . . .

Yuki asleep in a chair.

Miho places the film can upright on the floor in the middle of the hall and carefully approaches the rehearsal studio, stopping in the doorway to see . . .

The gun lying on the floor next to a half-empty bottle of whiskey.

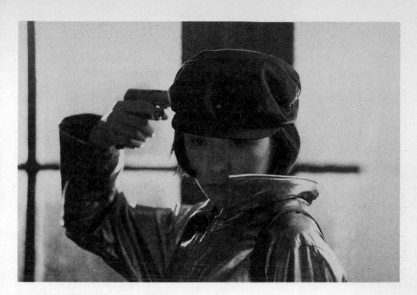

EXT. SCHOOL. SAME TIME

Tomo and Mochi pull up and hop out of their car.

INT. REHEARSAL STUDIO. SAME TIME

Miho approaches Yuki, carefully reaching out to grab the gun off the floor. But, as she is about to take it, Yuki's hand darts out and grips Miho's wrist.

Miho looks up to . . .

Yuki, who stares back at her, drunk, despairing, and dangerous.

Miho looks back down at the floor and grabs the gun with her free hand.

Meanwhile, downstairs, Mochi and Tomo enter the building.

Back upstairs, Miho struggles to cross the room and leave with the gun, while Yuki clings desperately to her arm, thrashing around wildly. Miho finally shakes her off and puts the gun to her own head.

Yuki lies sprawled on the floor, stunned.

Miho stares her down, strong, convicted, fed up, and impervious.

Yuki begins to cry.

Mochi mounts the steps to the second floor, while Tomo tries to get a candy bar from the vending machine in the downstairs hall.

Back in the rehearsal hall, Miho finally relaxes and lowers the gun from her head. She crosses the room to console Yuki, coming down over her just as she did in the dance rehearsal and embracing her tenderly.

She has forgotten, however, that she is still holding the gun, which is now pointing directly at her own face.

Mochi appears in the doorway, carefully stepping around the film can, which he considers dangerous. Tomo wanders past him, admiring the old school. Mochi now sees the two women huddled together in the dark studio and draws his gun.

As he observes them from the safety of the doorway, Tomo comes back, sees the film can, and give it a little kick with his boot.

The film can falls to the floor.

WHACK!!!

It startles the women. The gun goes off and Miho is thrown back on to the floor.

Yuki looks on in horror.

INT. HALLWAY. MOMENTS LATER

Miho staggers up the hall holding her face. She collapses at the top of the stairs and passes out. Tomo runs over, sees her face, and runs away.

INT. HOSPITAL. NIGHT

It's a noisy emergency room. Miho kicks and screams a lot. The Doctor and Nurse work quickly and have to shout.

> DOCTOR
>
> This is bad.
>> *(then, to nurse)*
>
> Wipe all this away.

The Nurse begins to clean Miho's face while the Doctor prepares an injection.

DOCTOR

I'm going to give you something for the pain. But this is going to be painful anyway.

NURSE
(*to Miho*)

Breathe.

The Doctor approaches.

DOCTOR

I'm going to have to inject the painkiller directly into the wounds.

NURSE

Just remember to breathe.

DOCTOR

There will be a number of injections.

He gives her one of these injections and she shrieks in pain. The Nurse tries to hold her still. The Doctor is frustrated.

Listen! I know! I know! I can't put you out! I need you to cooperate!

NURSE
(*to Miho*)

Think about something. Something specific.

INT. A BEDROOM. SOME OTHER DAY

Micho pictures a man's hand sliding over her thigh and up between her legs.

INT. HOSPITAL. SAME TIME

Slam back into the loud and violent operation room.

DOCTOR

This is bad.

NURSE
(*calling, off*)

More gauze!

INT. ANOTHER BEDROOM. SOME OTHER DAY

Miho leans back on the bed as an Older Man leans down over her and kisses her neck.

INT. HOSPITAL. SAME TIME

DOCTOR

Your entire upper lip is in three pieces. Can you feel that?

No answer. He goes on.

One of the tears goes right across your cheek. You can feel *that*, can't you?

INT. A THIRD BEDROOM. SOME OTHER DAY

A handsome Young Man lies on his stomach in bed. Miho leans down and kisses him, then pulls the sheets back to admire his naked body.

INT. HOSPITAL. SAME TIME

Miho screams. The Doctor is losing confidence.

DOCTOR
(*to Nurse*)

The painkiller is running right out of the wounds. There's no place for it to stay!

NURSE
(*to Miho*)

That's painkiller in your mouth right now. Not blood. Do you need to spit?

INT. A FOURTH BEDROOM. SOME OTHER DAY

Hal is sleeping with his arms around Miho. She is awake. She smiles when she discovers he still has his watch on.

She removes it and puts it on her own wrist.

86

She closes her eyes and goes to sleep.

INT. HOSPITAL. LATER THAT NIGHT

Miho sits on the edge of the operating table. Her face is all bandaged up and she looks like hell.

She sits there for a while, too weak to move.

Finally, she reaches back for her jacket. She feebly works her way into it, aching all over.

She pauses a moment, then slides herself off the table.

She's uncertain on her feet as she starts to move away towards the hall.

INT. HOSPITAL RECEPTION AREA. MOMENTS LATER

Miho comes down the hall to the lobby and pauses, uncertain.

She finds some change and moves to the pay-phone. She lifts the receiver and realizes she has no one to call. She hangs there a moment, lost, then she sees something across the waiting-room.

Hal is asleep in a seat across the large waiting-room, a half-empty can of beer in his hand, and his feet kicked up on top of his numerous film cans.

Miho watches him for a moment, then slowly lowers the receiver. She moves towards him.

He does not stir as she comes over, drops her bag and moves aside a film can. She collapses into the seat beside Hal, takes the beer can from his hand, and leans up against him. Finally, she takes his arm, places it around her shoulders, and closes her eyes.

The end.

CREDITS

True Fiction Pictures presents
in association with Pandora Films and Nippon Film Development &
Finance

FLIRT

A film by HAL HARTLEY

CAST

Harry	FRANK SCHENDLER
Boris, laborer #1	HANS MARTIN STIER
Peter, laborer #2	LARS RUDOLPH
Mike, laborer #3	JÖRG BIESTER
Mac, the Bartender	GERHARD SEVERIN
Barkeeper	SABINE SVOBODA
Model	SUSIE BICK
Photographer	AMINA GUSNER
Assistant	STEFAN KOLOSKO
Werner	JAKOB KLAFFKE
Greta's daughter	JOY KRAFT
Neighbor	BANO DOST
Man	HASAN ALI METE

TOKYO

Miho	MIHO NIKAIDOH
Naomi, Miho's friend	KUMIKO ISHIZUKA
Yuki, Ozu's wife	CHIKAKO HARA
Mr Ozu	TOSHIZO FUJIWARA
Mochi, policeman	MEIKYOH YAMADA
Tomo, younger policeman	MANSAKU IKEUCHI
Doctor	YUTAKA MATSUSHIGE
Nurse	TOMOKO FUJITA
Kazuko, jailbird #1	ERI YU
Shoko, jailbird #2	YURI ASO
Narumi, jailbird #3	NATSUMI MIZUNO
Hal, Miho's boyfriend	HAL HARTLEY
Hal's assistant	MASATOSHI NAGASE
Dancers	TETSUYA TABATA
	HIROFUMI NAKAGAWA
	MORITO IKEDA
	KENJI YAMAGUCHI
	JUNJI I JIMA
	TETSUSHI YAMAZAKI

a
TRUE FICTION
PANDORA FILM
NDF
co-production
with the support of
FILMBOARD BERLIN-BRANDENBURG Gmbh

● color ● 35mm ● 85 minutes ●
In English/German/Japanese
with English subtitles ● 1.1:66
A Cinepix Film Properties Release

Toronto Film Festival, 1995
New York Film Festival, 1995
Sundance Film Festival, 1996

Written and Directed by	HAL HARTLEY
Producer	TED HOPE
Executive Producers	REINHARD BRUNDIG
	SATORU ISEKI
	JEROME BROWNSTEIN
Cinematography	MICHAEL SPILLER
Original Music	NED RIFLE AND JEFF TAYLOR
Associate Producer	HISAMI KUROIWA
Associate Producer/New York	CARLEEN I. HSU
Production Services/Berlin	ZERO FILM
Line Producer	MARTIN HAGEMANN
Production Services/Tokyo	NEXUS NETWORK TOKYO
	TOSHIMORI IWAKI

CREW: NEW YORK, FEBRUARY 1993

First Assistant Director	Steve Appicella
Second Assistant Director	M J April
Script Supervisor	Adrienne Tien
Production Accountant	Joyce Hsieh
Production Coordinator	Craig Paull
Location Manager	Larry Ganem
Administrative Assistant	Ann Markel
Casting Directors	Billy Hopkins
	Suzanne Smith
Casting Associate	Diana Jaher
Extras Casting	Lila Mirochin
First Assistant Camera	Leah Schoenewolf
Second Assistant Camera	Ena Skuladottir
Still Photographer	Richard Ludwig
Additional Photographer	Mara Catalan
Key Grip	Paul Candrilli
Second Grip	Eric Klein
Third Grip	Sarah Black

Gaffer	W. Frank Stubblefield
	Dave Samuels
Best Boy Electric	Linda Phillips
Third Electric	Adrian Truini
Additional Electric	Teresa Ballard
	Cornelius Schutz-Kraft
Production Sound Mixer	Jeff Pullman
Boom Operator	Jeanne Gilliland
Costume Designer	Alexandra Welker
Wardrobe Assistant	Lila Mirochin
Make-Up Artist	Judy Chin
Assistant Make-Up	Marjorie Durand
Production Designer	Steven Rosenzweig
Art Director	Karin Wiesel
Set Decorator	Amy Tapper
Set Dresser	Jennifer Baime
Prop Master	Sarah Lavery
Second Props	Hope Litoff
Product Placement	Lisa Gossels
Art Assistants	Thierry Didonna
	Joey Garfield
	Jami Kibel
	David Shanker
Production Assistants	Jeff Frederick
	Alyssa Goldberg
	Rick Lange
	Jason Lowi
	Kendall McCarthy
	Cass O'Meara
	Tina Salomon
	Johnny Santiago
	Jacqui Sullivan
Craft Services	Allan McKinnon
Caterer	La Violette Fancy Foods
Parking Services	John Brentus
	Tom Patterson
Security	Scott Wyles
Transportation Captain	Christopher Fanning
Vehicles	Courier Car Rental
Camera Equipment	Ceco
Grip & Lighting Equipment	Northern Lights
Dailies Processing	DuArt Film & Video

Negative Cutters	Stan and Patricia Sztaba
Condom Dispenser	Barnett International

CREW: BERLIN, OCTOBER 1994

Production Manager	Roland Schmidt
First Assistant Director	Hans Schönherr
Assistant to the Director	Sarah Gross
Script Supervisor	Monika Von Manteuffel
Production Coordinator	Katrin Rohm
Location Manager	Michael Krüger
Casting Director	Christoph Rüter
Casting Extras	Mechthild Olliges
	Wolfgang Laubner
First Assistant Camera	Christoph Krauss
Second Assistant Camera	Nicolay Gutscher
Still Photographer	Christa Köfer
Grip	Vincent Botsch
Key Grip	Frank Stuck
Third Grip	Bernhard Keller
Gaffer	Helmut Prein
Best Boy Electric	Georg Nonnenmacher
Third Electrician	Andreas Müller
Sound Mixer	Norman Engel
Boom Operator	Frank Friedemann
Costume Designer	Ulla Gothe
Wardrobe Assistant	Ines Fritscher
Hair/Make Up Artist	Gabrielle Theurer
Art Director	Ric Schachtebeck
Set Decorator	Edgar Hinz
Prop Master	Lars Lange
Key Production Assistant	Edmund Müller
Production Assistants	Catherine Findeisen
	Brigitte Janus
Catering	Sarah Wiener's Tracking Catering
Parking Coordinators	Bloc Inc.
	Folker Greisner
	Greta Hartkopf
Drivers	Alexander Schubert
	Axel Scholz
Camera, Grip & Lighting Equipment	FGV Schmidle
Dailies Processing	Geyer-Werke GmbH

Dailies Supervisor	Hans-Joachim Rabs

CREW: TOKYO, MARCH 1995

Production Manager	Makiko Tomoda
First Assistant Director	Isao Yukisada
Assistant Directors	Shinichi Shimano
	Michael Baskett
Script Supervisor	Haruko Imamura
Assistant to Production Manager	Miki Kasamatsu
Production Liaison	Mark Higashino
Location Manager	Shouichi Takeuchi
Preparation Coordinators	Tsutomu Sakurai
	Kazutoshi Wadakura
Casting Director	Tsuyoshi Sugino
Casting Assistant	Miwa Ishiguro
Choreographer	Yoshito Ohno
First Assistant Camera	Storn Norpsan Peterson
Second Assistant Camera	Wong On Lim
Still Photographer	Mark Higashino
Assistant Still Photographer	Akira Utsunomiya
Key Grip	Fumisada Kaneshiro
Best Boy Grip	Yasunobu Isa
Gaffer	Toshi Ozawa
Best Boy Electric	Katsunori Saito
Electrician	Kenji 'Buchie' Mizobuchi
Generator Operator	Tetsuya Aoki
Production Sound Mixer	Osamu Takizawa
Boom Operator	Osamu Shimizu
Wardrobe Supervisor	Takako Hamai
Hair & Makeup Artist	Midori Onuma
Assistant Hair & Makeup Artist	Masayo Ishikawa
Art Director	Tomoyuki Maruo
Set Dectorator	Fumiaki Suzaka
Prop Master	China Hayashi
Assistant Prop Master	Naohino Ohno
Second Props	Miki Kasamatsu
Production Assistants	Hiroshi Oni shi
	Narito Shimizu
	Kotaro Tanabe
Intem	Masaki Tokumi
Honorary Transportation Captain	Satoru Iseki

94

Camera Grip & Lighting Equipment	Sanwa Cine Equipment Rental Co. Ltd.
Dailies Processing	Imagica
Dailies Supervisor	Harup Kakinuma
Dailies Time	Hideo Yamaoka

POST-PRODUCTION

Supervising Sound Editor	Steve Hamilton
Sound Editor	Steve Silkensen
	Jennifer Ralston
Editor/New York	Steve Hamilton
Assistant Editor/New York	Meg Bowles
Assistant Editor/Berlin	Susan Littenberg
Editing Intern/Berlin	Tommy Tsuda
Assistant Editor/Tokyo	Sherrie Liu
	Joe Cimino
Post Production Supervisor	Kelly Miller
Translation	Almut Fitzgerald
	Yoko Umezawa
Post Production Mixer	Reilly Steele
Post Production Facilities	Spin Cycle Post
	Sound One
Titles and Optical Effects	REI Media Group
Answer Prints	DuArt Film & Video
Timer	David Pultz
Negative Cutter	Noëlle Penraat
Legal Counsel	Roger Kass & W. Wilder Knight II
Production Legal Counsel/Tokyo	Keiji Iwaki
Insurance	Disc Insurance
	Cohen Insurance
Music Guest Performers	Lydia Kavanagh
	Mark Bailey

95